The Plain Truth About Christmas

Where did the world get Christmas? . . . from the Bible? Here are the astonishing facts which may shock you! Test yourself. How much do you know of the origin of the Christmas tree—of "Santa Claus"—of the mistletoe—of the holly wreath—of the custom of exchanging gifts?

Chapter one: Text by Clayton D. Steep
© 1981 Worldwide Church of God
Chapter two: Text by Keith W. Stump
© 1985 Worldwide Church of God
Chapter three: Text by John Halford
© 1985 Worldwide Church of God
Chapter four: © 1986 Worldwide Church of God
Cover photo: G.A. Belluche Jr.—*PT*
All Rights Reserved
Printed in U.S.A.

ISBN 1-55825-103-0

Table of Contents

Chapter 1
CHRISTMAS 2,000 YEARS
BEFORE CHRIST! 1

Chapter 2
JESUS' BIRTH—THE UNTOLD STORY 5

Chapter 3
SO YOU'RE NOT
KEEPING CHRISTMAS? 14

Chapter 4
QUESTIONS AND ANSWERS 18

CHRISTMAS 2,000 YEARS BEFORE CHRIST

It was that festive season again. The little children were filled with anticipation and excitement. The whole family was busy putting up decorations. Boughs of holly and evergreen were assembled and placed about the house. The mistletoe was hung. A tree was chosen and decorated with sparkling trinkets and ornaments.

It was a season of giving and receiving presents, a time to sing songs, admire all the pretty lights and burn the Yule log. There were to be parades with special floats, sumptuous meals and merrymaking.

A modern Christmas celebration? Not at all!

At the end of December and the beginning of January all these festive celebrations were taking place in various nations of Europe centuries before Jesus Christ was born!

An "Old-fashioned" Christmas

Where Christmas customs came from is really no secret. You can read the origins of Christmas customs in encyclopedias and other reference works. The *Encyclopedia Britannica,* for example, draws attention to these facts: "Christmas customs are an evolution from times that long antedate the Christian period—a descent from seasonal, pagan, religious and national practices, hedged about with legend and tradition" (15th edition, article "Christmas").

In ancient times, many people, realizing their dependence upon the sun for light, heat and the growing of crops, watched the sun's yearly course through the heavens with deep interest. At different seasons, feasts and celebrations were observed to help the solar orb on its way.

The end of December was an especially significant time in the Northern Hemisphere. The days were short. The sun was at its lowest point. Special festivals of thanksgiving and encouragement to the sun were celebrated.

When, at the winter solstice, the days began to lengthen, there was great celebration lasting into the first part of January. The reason was that the sun—the light of the world—had been reborn!

Such festivities, once meant to honor the sun and its god, were freely adopted by the spreading and increasingly popular "Christian" religion. Why not, in the same way, honor Jesus—the real light of the world (even though he was not actually born in December as we shall discover in the next chapter)? Through the centuries different combinations of customs developed in different nations. But the origin of the celebrations goes back at least 4,000 years.

Trees, Candles and Holiday Cheer

The modern Christmas tree is supposed to have originated in German lands in the Middle Ages. But long before that, the ancestors of the Germans customarily decorated their homes with lights and greenery at the winter festival.

Since evergreens were green throughout the dead of winter, the ancient Germans looked upon them as especially imbued with life. It was in honor of the tree spirit or the spirit of growth and fertility that greenery was a prominent part of ancient pagan winter celebrations.

The Romans trimmed trees with trinkets and toys at that time of the year. The Druids tied gilded apples to tree branches. It is difficult to trace back exactly where the legend first gained popularity, but to certain peoples an evergreen decorated with orbs and other fruit-like objects symbolized the tree of life in the Garden of Eden.

Branches of holly and mistletoe were likewise revered. Not only did these plants remain green through the winter months, but they actually bore fruit at that time, once again honoring the spirits of fertility. Still today, catching someone under a branch of mistletoe can serve as a convenient springboard for romantic activity. Few people stop to wonder what in the world such strange customs have to do with the birth of Jesus.

The ancients lit festive fires in late December to encourage the sun, just as Christmas bonfires, candles and other lights burn today at the same time of the year. Use of the "Yule log," part of the "Yuletide" season, hearkens back to the ritual burning of a carefully chosen log by the Druids. The word *yule* comes from the old Anglo-Saxon word *hweol*, meaning "wheel," a wheel being a symbol for the sun.

> *Few stop to wonder what such strange customs have to do with Jesus' birth.*

You thought the Christmas shopping spree was a 20th-century phenomenon?

Listen to how fourth-century writer Libanius described end-of-the-year gift-giving and partying in the ancient non-Christian Roman Empire: "Everywhere may be seen ... well-laden tables ... The impulse to spend seizes everyone. He who through the whole year has taken pleasure in saving ... becomes suddenly extravagant.... A stream of presents pours itself out on all sides" (quoted in *Christmas in Ritual and Tradition*).

Of all times in the year, it was indeed the season to be jolly. Then, as now, in a constant round of partying, it was common—yes, expected—to seek the "spirit" of the season in whatever intoxicating drink was at hand. Drunkenness was widespread. Fortunately, however, the modes of transportation in those days did not lend themselves to the high rate of drunken-driver-induced traffic fatalities that are part of the Christmas season in many nations today.

An important part of the pagan harvest festivities—beginning in October-November with what has become Halloween—involved good and bad spirits. In many lands, mythical visitors—usually bringers of good or evil—became the center of attention in the winter season. Through blending ancient legends with traditions about saints, certain similar figures emerged.

And Santa Claus?

We recognize them today in different nations as Santa Claus, Father Christmas, St. Nicholas, St. Martin, the Weihnachtsmann, Père Noël. Whatever name is used, all these winter visitors fulfill a similar role.

These fictional persons—"Christianizations" of the pagan Germanic deities—perpetuate certain folk rituals wherein varying degrees of rewards and punishments were dealt out to celebrants. Through the centuries these customs came to be centered around children.

It is not hard to see a connection between Santa using the chimney, the shoes and stockings hung by the fireplace and the ancient superstitions about hearth spirits. The fireplace served as the natural entrance and exit of the gods of fire and solar gods when they visited homes. For thousands of years, especially among the Chinese, it was customary to sweep and scour the house in preparation for the visit of the hearth spirit.

Each year, dressed in a pointed fiery red cap and red jacket, this fire-god traveled from the distant heavens to visit homes and distribute favors or punishments. Today he is welcomed in the Western world each Christmas season by young and old alike.

Popular Christmas customs, as we can see, plainly reflect non-Christian legends and practices. The logical question to ask is: What is there that is *Christian* about Christmas? Did you know, for example, that some of the very Christmas customs observed today were once banned by the Catholic Council of Rome, the English Parliament and the Puritans of New England? More importantly, what does the Bible say about Christmas? Should a Christian have anything to do with such holidays?

JESUS' BIRTH— THE UNTOLD STORY

Was Jesus born in December? If not, when was he born? And in what year? Any way, what difference does it make? These are questions often asked. It is time they were answered!

In late December of each year, thousands of tourists flock into the small town of Bethlehem in the Judean Hills south of Jerusalem to participate in annual Christmas celebrations there. Some make the 6-mile journey from Jerusalem on foot. Upon arrival, they crowd with silent awe into the paved expanse of Manger Square in front of the revered Church of the Nativity, built over the traditional site of Jesus' birth.

Inevitably, some of these tourists arrive in Israel unprepared. They have not thoroughly studied their guidebooks. As they step off their plane, they receive a real *shock!*

November through early March is "winter" in Israel! The weather gets cold, especially at night. Often it rains—or even snows! Yet many arrive in Israel carrying luggage bulging with summer attire, reasoning that it is always hot and arid in the Middle East. So they hurriedly purchase coats and sweaters in Tel Aviv or Jerusalem so they can make their pilgrimage down to Bethlehem.

Nevertheless, most of those who stand in Manger Square on December 25 each year—prepared and unprepared alike—

fail to perceive the message being proclaimed by the very weather around them!

Notice this plain testimony of your Bible: On the day of Jesus' birth "there were in the same country shepherds abiding in the field, keeping watch over their flock by night" (Luke 2:8).

The shepherds were living out in the open fields, tending their flock through the night. The point?

Ask any biblical scholar, or any modern Israeli: This *never* could have occurred in Judea in the month of December—nor even in November, or late October as far as that is concerned!

In ancient times as today, shepherds brought their flocks in from the fields and penned them in shelters *not later than the middle of October!* This was necessary to protect them from the cold, rainy season that usually followed that date. (The Bible itself makes it clear that winter in Palestine is a rainy season; see Ezra 10:9, 13; Song of Solomon 2:11.)

Yet Luke 2:8 tells us that at the time of Jesus' birth, the shepherds were yet *abiding* in the fields—*by night,* at that! They had not yet brought their flocks home to the sheepfolds. Clearly the cold, rainy season had not yet commenced.

Thus, on the basis of Luke's testimony alone, we see that Jesus could have been born *no later than* mid-October—when the weather is still pleasant at Bethlehem. A December 25 nativity is too late!

More Proof

Additional biblical evidence lends further support to the foregoing conclusion.

Luke 1:24-38 informs us that the virgin Mary miraculously became pregnant with Jesus when her cousin Elizabeth was six months pregnant with a child who would later be known as John the Baptist. Jesus, then, would have been born six months after John.

If we could know the time of John's birth, we could then simply add six months and know the time of Jesus' birth.

Does the Bible reveal the general time of John's birth?

Notice: Elizabeth's husband Zacharias was a priest at the Temple in Jerusalem. Luke 1:5 records that Zacharias was

according to B.C. and A.D. was devised hundreds of years after Jesus' birth. It was invented in the sixth century A.D. by a monk in Italy named Dionysius Exiguus.

This Dionysius misunderstood the time of the reign of Herod the Great, king of Judea. So he reckoned the birth of Jesus to have occurred in December of the year 753 A.U.C. (*ab urbe condita*—"from the foundation of the city [of Rome]"). In past ages, time was often reckoned using the founding of Rome as the starting point for counting.

Thus, in Dionysius' new system, January 1, 754 A.U.C., became January 1, A.D. 1 (*anno Domini,* "in the year of the Lord"). That is, he assumed Jesus was born on December 25, just a week before January 1, A.D. 1.

Error Later Discovered

Later, it was discovered that Dionysius had been incorrect in his reckoning of the reign of Herod and hence of the commencement of the Christian era. Jesus had been born some years *earlier* than Dionysius had thought. But by then, the new chronology was in general use and it was too late to change! It has continued in use throughout most of the world to the present day.

With that understanding, we can now proceed to determine the year of Jesus' birth. There are several ways of doing so.

Notice, first, this ancient prophecy from the book of Daniel:

> *I*n ancient times as today, shepherds brought their flocks in from the fields . . . not later than the middle of October!

"Know therefore and understand, that from the going forth of the commandment to restore and to build Jerusalem unto the Messiah the Prince shall be seven weeks, and threescore and two weeks . . ." (Dan. 9:25).

The commandment or decree to restore and build Jerusalem was made in the seventh year of the reign of Artaxerxes I, king of ancient Persia (see Ezra 7:8)—according to the autumn-to-autumn reckoning of the Jews, in 457 B.C. The archangel Gabriel told Daniel that there would be a total of 69 prophetic weeks from that time until the public appearance of the Messiah.

Sixty-nine weeks is equivalent to 483 days (69 x 7). A day of prophetic fulfillment is a year in actual time (Num. 14:34; Ezek. 4:6). So 483 prophetic days (69 prophetic weeks) is *483 years.*

Simple arithmetic now takes over. Four-hundred-eighty-three years from 457 B.C. (the year of the decree) brings us to A.D. 27—the year when Jesus, the Messiah, began his public ministry. (In calculating this, be aware that you must add 1 to compensate for the fact that there is no year zero.)

Now consider further: It is generally understood that Jesus entered upon his ministry in the *autumn* of the year, immediately after his baptism. (His ministry lasted 3½ years, ending in the *spring,* at Passover time.) In Luke 3:23 we learn that Jesus was "about thirty years of age" when he began his ministry. If he was about 30 years old in the autumn of A.D. 27, then he must have been *born* in the end of summer or early autumn, and in *4* B.C.! (Remember, there is no year zero.)

It thus stands clearly revealed from Daniel's prophecy that Jesus was born in 4 B.C. But there is yet further proof!

Herod's Eclipse

Students of the Bible recognize that Jesus was born *before* the death of Herod the Great (Matt. 2:15, 19). When did Herod die?

The first century A.D. Jewish historian Flavius Josephus, in *Antiquities of the Jews* (book XVII, chapter vi), tells of an eclipse of the moon late in Herod's reign. The authoritative *Solar and Lunar Eclipses of the Ancient Near East* by Kudlek and Mickler reveals that the lunar eclipse in question occurred on March 13, 4 B.C.

Continuing with Josephus' account, we discover that sometime after the eclipse, Herod—afflicted with a painful and loathsome disease—went beyond the river Jordan to bathe himself in hot springs there. The cures he undertook were unsuccessful. His condition worsened and he returned to Jericho. There, in a wild rage, he plotted the deaths of many prominent Jews. He also ordered his own son, Antipater, slain. All these events required some months.

Josephus further reveals (chapter ix) that Herod's death occurred sometime before a spring Passover. This Passover would have been 13 months after the eclipse, or the Passover of April, 3 B.C. This confirms our previously calculated 4 B.C. birthdate for Jesus.

Further corroborating this, Josephus also records (XVII, viii, 1) that at his death, Herod had reigned 37 years since he had been declared king by the Romans. That had occurred in 40 B.C., a fact that Dionysius overlooked. Herod's death therefore took place late in 4 B.C.—more specifically, according to a Jewish tradition, on the seventh day of the lunar month Kislev in the Hebrew calendar (equivalent to November/December on the Roman calendar)—shortly after Jesus' birth in the early autumn of 4 B.C.

This is the *only* date that is consistent with all the provable facts!

The "Star" of Bethlehem

A word is necessary at this point about the celebrated "Star of Bethlehem" (Matt. 2) that guided the wise men (Greek, *Magi*) across the deserts of the East to Bethlehem.

Scholars have tried to pinpoint the date of Jesus' birth by means of astronomical calculations related to the appearance of this mysterious "star." For centuries, theologians and astronomers have debated this perplexing question.

Dozens of theories exist purporting to explain what this "star" actually was and when it appeared. Some hold it was a comet. Others postulate a nova (exploding star). Still others say it was a meteor, or a planet, or a conjunction of two or more planets. (A conjunction takes place when planets appear, from our earthly viewpoint, to briefly become a single bright object as their paths cross the sky.) Dates for proposed celestial phenomena usually range from 7 B.C. to 2 B.C.

But the heart and core of the star controversy goes beyond matters of astronomy. To one who believes that the Bible is the Word of God and is to be taken at face value, the account of the star in Matthew's gospel can have only one explanation. It was clearly and incontrovertibly a *miracle,* of *supernatural*—not natural—origin!

What natural phenomenon in the heavens—whether comet, meteor, exploding star or planet—could "go before" the Magi and "stand over" a specific house to *precisely pinpoint* it (Matt. 2:9-11)? And if it was attributable to a nonmiraculous agency, how can we account that it appeared and reappeared to the Magi and apparently went generally unnoticed by others?

Natural explanations are sheer astronomical foolishness! If the biblical account cannot be accepted in *all* its details, why should anyone believe it has any merit at all?

The star was clearly a special miracle of God, of divine origin, defying all the proposed natural explanations of liberal scholarship. It is quite possible that the Star

> *The star was clearly a special miracle of God, of divine origin, defying all the proposed natural explanations of liberal scholarship.*

of Bethlehem was simply an *angel* sent to lead the Magi to Jesus, since the Bible often symbolically uses stars to signify angels (Job 38:7; Jude 13; Rev. 1:20; 9:1; 12:4; et al.).

In Jesus' Name?

We have seen the proof that Jesus was born in the early autumn, not in the winter. But, some will ask, what difference does it make? Is it not *the thought* that counts?

Each December, articles inevitably appear in newspapers and magazines pointing out the ancient origins of today's Christmas customs. All authorities agree that the customs surrounding Christmas—the Christmas tree, mistletoe, holly wreaths, yule logs, stockings on the hearth, exchanging gifts and so on—were practiced in connection with pagan religious celebrations *centuries before* the birth of Jesus. *None* are of Christian origin! Anciently, December 25 was the date of the pagan Roman Brumalia, the final day of the popular week-long Saturnalia celebration, celebrated in honor of the god

Saturn. It was the day of the "invincible sun"—a winter solstice festival.

"Christmas" was not among the earliest festivals of the Church. It was not until the mid-fourth century that Pope Julius I decreed December 25 to be Christmas ("Christ-Mass") Day. He sought to overshadow the popular Brumalia by imparting "Christian" connotations to the day.

But again, some will ask: What is so wrong with borrowing some of those early customs and using them to honor Jesus? May we not continue to celebrate December 25, as long as we do it *in Jesus' name?*

Can pagan practices be "Christianized" in this way?

More than 34 centuries ago, the rebellious children of Israel fashioned a pagan idol—a golden calf—in the wilderness (Ex. 32). It was the god Apis, the sacred Egyptian bull deity worshiped at Memphis on the Nile. Aaron declared that the pagan, Egyptian rites by which the Israelites worshiped the calf were "a feast to the Lord" (verse 5).

Did God feel honored? Did he approve of their using pagan customs to worship him?

Absolutely not! It was a *great sin* (verse 21), and 3,000 paid with their lives (verse 28)! They had *deceived* themselves that what they were doing was right.

We are commanded not to seek to worship God with customs borrowed from other religions (Deut. 12:29-32). "Learn not the way of the heathen," God declares (Jer. 10:2).

True Christians never meet paganism half way. Pagan worship—whether "in Jesus' name" or not—*remains* pagan worship! Christianity mixed with paganism is not Christianity at all. Righteousness has no fellowship with unrighteousness (II Cor. 6:14). God simply will not accept that type of false "worship."

If God had wanted us to observe Christ's birthday, he would have given us the exact date and specific instructions on how to observe it. But he has not! Christmas is an invention of *man,* issuing from pagan worship.

SO YOU'RE NOT KEEPING CHRISTMAS?

S O YOU have decided it's time to make some changes. This year you and your family are (sssh—don't let the neighbors know!)—not going to keep Christmas!

But it isn't quite as easy as that though, is it? Christmas has become so much a part of most people's lives that not to observe it can mean a major disruption. No Christmas cards. What will Aunt Tess think? No relatives over for Christmas dinner. No decorations. No lights or Santa Claus. You'll have to try to avoid the office party, and you'd better write to the school explaining that you don't want little Fred to play an angel in the Christmas play. And no tree.

I remember the first time we didn't have a tree. It had always been a feature in our house. We would go to a lot of trouble to decorate it beautifully, and then put it in the front window for all to see. A good-looking tree was a status symbol in our neighborhood and, though I do say it myself, ours was one of the best and most impressive.

But we noticed in the Bible where God made some pretty pointed remarks about decorated trees. Check it for yourself in Jeremiah 10:3-4. God said it was a futile, pagan custom—a clear case of worshiping Christ in vain. So—no tree. Even though we knew we had done the right thing, we really missed that tree. The neighbors all had them, sparkling in their windows, but our window remained dark.

We missed it so much that we cheated a bit. We put up a few decorations—not a tree, mind you, just a few bits and pieces to make the place look more cheerful. And we had a Christmas dinner, only we didn't call it that. It was only a "celebration."

We felt guilty about it, because we knew we had compromised. It was just that the old way seemed so comfortable, and without a tree and all the rest of the paraphernalia, Christmas just didn't seem like—er, Christmas.

Jesus Christ knew this would happen. He explained to his disciples that they would indeed miss some aspects of the old way of life, and that even as they learned the truth from him they would look back nostalgically from time to time.

Jesus taught an important lesson in Luke 5:36-39: "No one puts a piece from a new garment on an old one; otherwise the new makes a tear, and also the piece that was taken out of the new does not match the old" (verse 36).

Any seamstress understands that. New, unshrunk material cannot be used to patch old, worn garments. When it shrinks, it will tear the old cloth even worse than before.

Jesus' second analogy is not quite so easy for us to follow in the 20th century: "And no one puts new wine into old wineskins; or else the new wine will burst the wineskins and be spilled, and the wineskins will be ruined. But new wine must be put into new wineskins" (verses 37-38).

In New Testament times glass bottles were rare, so wine was often transported in animal skins, usually from goats. They made a strong, airtight and moisture-proof container, but you had to be careful. New wine that had not finished fermenting gave off gas that would expand the skins. A new wineskin had some "give" to it, and would allow for the expansion. But old, used skins lost their elasticity. They would burst. The wine would be spilled and the wineskin ruined.

But why tell people that? Jesus Christ's business was not to give the multitude helpful household hints. Jesus was using a familiar situation to teach an aspect of Christian living.

Withdrawal symptoms

When someone begins to understand the teachings of the Bible, it is a totally new experience—unlike anything he or she has ever known—like new wine or an unused piece of cloth.

Now, what most of us do is try to fit this new truth into our old way of life. That is only natural, because it is hard to change, and no one likes to admit having been wrong. The old way of life is familiar and comfortable, and we want to hang on to as much of it as possible.

How about you? Perhaps you have fond memories of the Easter sunrise service, the fun of Halloween and those beautiful candlelight carol services down at the old family church. The truth comes smashing into inherited religious ideas and preconceived notions of right and wrong. It challenges comfortable beliefs, making you question things you have always done.

This new way—even if it is right—sometimes seems like an unwelcome intruder, and you find yourself resenting it.

Jesus warned us that that could happen: "And no one, having drunk old wine, immediately desires new; for he says, 'The old is better' " (verse 39).

It is not surprising that so many people, even though they acknowledge the truth, still prefer to cling to their old beliefs. Or perhaps they do as my family did when we met the truth halfway, with a sort of "unChristmas" celebration.

We didn't enjoy our "unChristmas." You never can if you know that you are compromising with what is right. We were trying to put our new wine in the old bottle, and we spoiled everything.

> *It is not surprising that so many people, even though they acknowledge the truth, still prefer to cling to their old beliefs.*

Don't make that mistake. If you are beginning to understand what it means to be a real Christian, realize that it is going to demand positive action on your part. You can't have it both ways, observing this world's customs and still expecting the blessing of the world tomorrow.

"Why do you call Me 'Lord, Lord,' and do not the things which I say?" Jesus thundered (Luke 6:46). He expects total commitment. He demands that we come out of the Babylon of confusion that characterizes so much religion today.

So along with the excitement of learning new truth comes the responsibility of making some painful decisions. Don't compromise. God does not want to take from us anything that is good. His way of life is filled with exciting experiences that mean something and lead somewhere, not empty, senseless and often very expensive rituals.

As you take the plunge and follow God's way of life, you will begin to miss the "old wine" less and less. You will see it for what it is—a hollow counterfeit of the real thing.

God is showing you the way to freedom from all that. Instead of looking back at the fraudulent ways of this world, you will begin to anticipate the excitement of helping others learn the truth in the world tomorrow.

QUESTIONS AND ANSWERS

EACH YEAR our Personal Correspondence Department answers numerous inquiries regarding the holiday season. Here are some answers to some of the most frequently asked questions. If you have a question regarding the Christmas holiday and it has not been answered here, please feel free to write our Personal Correspondence Department at our address nearest you. They will be glad to help you.

So Christmas is based on pagan traditions and myths. What is wrong with borrowing some of those customs and using them to honor Jesus on his birthday?

If we are supposed to celebrate Jesus' birthday, why doesn't the Bible give us the date of that event? Elsewhere in the Scriptures, when God revealed certain days he wanted his people to observe, no room was left for doubt as to when those days occurred.

The instructions were specific because God wanted his people to observe those particular days. Why, then, the silence as to which day Christ was born?

But an even more important point to consider is this: When Jesus' name is applied to borrowed pagan ideas and practices, does Jesus really feel honored? After all, it was Jesus himself who told his people Israel not to seek to worship him with customs borrowed from other religions (Deut. 12:29-32). Time and again he made it clear through his prophets that he wanted his people to remain "cleansed . . . of everything pagan" (Neh. 13:30, *Revised Authorized Version*).

Even though I have ceased to celebrate Christmas, is there anything wrong in continuing to exchange gifts out of the motive of giving rather than wanting to follow pagan customs?

There is nothing wrong with giving to others. Part of God's overall purpose for our existence is that we learn to give instead of seeking to get. But a Christian needs to be careful about giving a gift around Christmas time.

The reason? Christians are to be lights to the world. They must set the example of righteous living. To engage in gift giving with those who are celebrating Christmas may give the appearance to them that you are participating right along with them in Christmas festivities.

God tells us to come out of the religious system of this world and to be "separate" (II Cor. 6:14-18). How can a person be separate from such goings on and continue at the same time to dabble in them?

Why not give gifts at other times of the year when they will be appreciated as spontaneously sincere and heartfelt?

How do I tell my friends and relatives that I no longer wish to exchange presents?

With a smile! That's right. Show firmness, yet at the same time be relaxed and friendly about it.

One of the biggest mistakes you can make is to come across as a religious fanatic fired up with purple-veined emotion on the subject. There's no need to make friends and relatives feel condemned and guilty by what you say. Your example will be testimony enough to them.

Most of them haven't the faintest idea where Christmas customs came from or why they are following them. They're just doing what everyone around them does.

Many of the problems arising from the Christmas season can be resolved if you apply three principles:

(1) *Stress your objection to the commercialism of the*

season. Immediately you have everyone, with the possible exception of some shopkeepers and commercial interests, on your side.

Who can deny that Christmas is a crassly commercial holiday, that it is budget-bustingly expensive? Who would not—especially as general economic conditions worsen —rather spend the money on more needful items, like maybe heating the house or buying winter clothing? Who does not dread the wearisome Christmas shopping experience, the crowds, the time-consuming uncertainty as to what to buy for whom?

All you have to say is you've had enough of it, that when you give a gift you want to do it spontaneously instead of as a slave to some custom. After the initial shock wears off, most people will respect your stand and secretly wish they had the courage to do likewise. Some, in fact, heartened by your example, may do just that!

(2) *Maintain a sense of humor.* Let's face it, cutting trees down and then setting them back up loaded with ornaments, the whole gift-trading rigmarole, the thought of an overweight, bearded individual decked out in flamboyant red and traveling through the air in a sled or some other conveyance when he is not slithering up and down someone's chimney—these and so many other traditions are ridiculous. Feel free to point that out. Who can deny it?

(3) *Put the burden of proof on those who are celebrating Christmas.* It's not that there isn't overwhelming proof to back you up in your decision to cease celebrating Christmas. There certainly is. But most people have neither the time nor the interest for a detailed explanation. So shift the burden of proof to them.

Say, in effect, "If you can show me where the Bible says I ought to observe Christmas, or where it says early Christians celebrated Jesus' birthday, then I will celebrate it also!"

The discussion will probably end very suddenly at that point. Of course, if the person to whom you are speaking shows an obvious interest in learning about the real origin of Christmas, you should be prepared to give an appropriate answer.

What happens if someone gives me a gift anyway? Should I return it?

If a person is testing you to see how deeply rooted are your religious convictions, returning the gift is a proper response.

On the other hand, in cases where the person sincerely doesn't know or comprehend your stand, a polite note of thanks for the gift and a brief statement that you no longer observe the Christmas holiday may be sufficient.

By the way, you will find that most people will stop giving you Christmas gifts anyway after a year or two of not receiving a gift from you in return.

My friends and relatives continue to send me Christmas cards. Should I write back to each of them and explain that I have quit celebrating Christmas?

A brief note to that effect may be in order. As with gifts, most people will cease sending Christmas cards when they stop getting them in return.

What do I tell my children now that they will no longer be receiving presents at Christmas?

Why not tell them the truth? Why not tell them that you have come to understand that the world is wrong in its observance of Christmas and that you are going to do God's will because it is better than Christmas?

Be sure to emphasize the positive side—that God's way is better than Christmas. As proof of this, tell your children you are going to give gifts to them throughout the year because you love them all year long, not just on Christmas day. That, in turn, is precisely what they can tell their friends who will be showing off their Christmas gifts.

It is important not to leave a void in your children's lives by removing Christmas observance and putting nothing in its place. Arrange special activities with them often, and especially centering around the Holy Days God has ordained in the Scriptures—the days he does want us to observe. (For more information, write for our free booklet *Pagan Holidays or God's Holy Days—Which?*)

Is there anything I can do to prevent my child from having to participate in Christmas activities at school?

One of the most important steps you as a Christian parent can take is to discuss the subject with the children's teachers, addressing the problem ahead of time. Politely inform the teachers involved that you do not observe certain holidays and that you do not want to have your children take part in celebrations centering around those days.

Seek to avoid, as much as possible, leaving a teacher in a difficult situation with children to teach but not knowing what to have them do while others, for example, are drawing Santas. You can advise that your children may draw winter scenes or snowmen instead of things immediately associated with Christmas. If the class is having a Christmas party perhaps you could offer to come to school and take your children home that afternoon to relieve the teacher from having to find something else for them to do. In any case, try to be very cooperative with school officials. Above all, ask God for wisdom and grace and favor in their sight.

Your children themselves, especially as they get older, will be a determining factor as to whether they become involved in worldly religious holiday activities at school or elsewhere away from home. You can't be with them every minute.

This underlines the absolute need to provide positive instruction at home. If children are convinced in their own minds that they should not participate in certain activities, much of the battle is already won.

It is a standard policy for the company where I work to give all employees a Christmas bonus. Should I accept this bonus?

Bonuses given at the end of the year are usually not considered as Christmas gifts. They are often given in gratitude for work done throughout the preceding year. It is logical to wait until the end of the year before giving such a bonus, and Christmas seems to be as good an occasion as any.

Most large companies are not interested one way or the other in the personal convictions of their employees and, when that's the case, there is no reason to refuse the bonus.

If you are working for a smaller company where you know your employer personally, it may be advisable to mention to him or her that you don't celebrate Christmas. If he or she wants to give you the bonus regardless, as simply a gift or token of appreciation, you can accept it with a clear conscience.

Some relatives have invited me to their house for dinner on Christmas Day. Should I refuse the invitation?

Not necessarily. It depends on the nature of the occasion. Since you understand the truth about Christmas, to you the day will be just another ordinary day of the year. And to you the simple fact of eating a meal with others on that day is no different from eating one with them on any other day.

What matters in this case, though, is how your relatives will regard the occasion. If they look on the meal as part of Christmas festivities and place religious significance upon it, then you would be out of place there. Your attendance could give the impression that you are observing Christmas with them or, if they know about your beliefs, that you are willing to compromise on your beliefs. On the other hand, if the meal is merely a convenient opportunity for a family get-together, and there is no objectionable connotation placed upon the meal, then it might be all right to accept the invitation.

Better be prepared to answer some questions, though, because sooner or later the conversation is sure to focus on why you don't observe Christmas.

What should I say when someone wishes me "Merry Christmas"?

It is often sufficient to respond with a question such as "Where has this last year gone?" or "It's that time of year again, isn't it?" or "Do you think it is going to snow?" or even a parting statement on an entirely unrelated subject such as "Good-bye now" or "Have a good day!" The surprising fact is that few individuals will even notice that you haven't wished "Merry Christmas" in return.

At other times, a smile and a "Thank you" (meaning you are grateful for their concern) may be more appropriate.

"And why call ye me Lord, Lord, and do not the things which I say?"

Luke 6:46

Jesus Christ made it clear that genuine Christianity is more than just a verbal confession, however sincere.

As He said, "Not everyone that says unto me, 'Lord, Lord,' shall enter into the kingdom of heaven" (Matt. 7:21).

Well, who will find salvation then? What is God looking for? Is regular church attendance enough? How about a good attitude and a friendly smile? What really makes someone a Christian?

This free booklet *What Is a Real Christian?* will help you discover the answer. No question could be more important to those seeking a true relationship with God.

To receive your free copy of *What Is a Real Christian?* send your request to one of our addresses listed on the last page of this booklet.

A Unique Cours
Understanding

Have you found it difficult—even impossible—to understand what the Bible says? The Ambassador College Bible Correspondence Course can help you begin to comprehend the Bible as never before. More than 2,000,000 people have enrolled in this unique course!

These informative, eye-opening lessons make plain the answers to the "unanswerable" problems facing millions today. They explain the very purpose of human life. You will study the plain truths of your Bible!

You will learn the truth about the purpose of life, about what Bible prophecy says concerning world events today, about the God-inspired way to true happiness. All these topics and more are presented in step-by-step detail. A different major subject is explored in each monthly lesson.

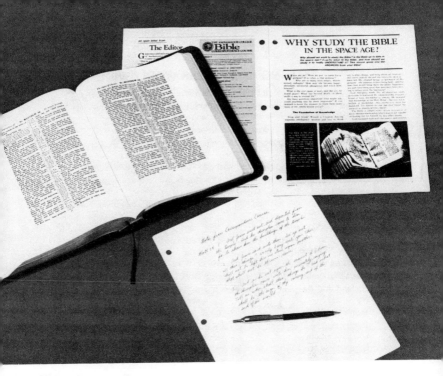

n Bible

And the Bible itself is the only textbook you will need.

You will find each lesson richly rewarding, and periodic quizzes will help you evaluate your progress. There is no tuition fee or obligation—these lessons are absolutely free! Why not request a sample lesson? Send your request in the reply envelope or write to our address nearest you.

Free of Charge

Just mail the reply envelope stitched into this booklet.

MAILING ADDRESSES WORLDWIDE

United States: Worldwide Church of God, Pasadena, California 91123

United Kingdom, Europe (except as listed) and Middle East: The Plain Truth, P.O. Box 111, Borehamwood, Herts, England WD6 1LU

Canada: Worldwide Church of God, P.O. Box 44, Station A, Vancouver, B.C. V6C 2M2

Canada (French language): Le Monde à Venir, B.P. 121, Succ. A, Montreal, P. Q. H3C 1C5

Mexico: Institución Ambassador, Apartado Postal 5-595, 06502 México D.F.

South America: Institución Ambassador, Apartado Aéreo 11430, Bogotá 1, D.E., Colombia

Caribbean: Worldwide Church of God, G.P.O. Box 6063, San Juan, Puerto Rico 00936-6063

France: Le Monde à Venir, B.P. 64, 75662 Paris Cédex 14, France

Switzerland: Le Monde à Venir, Case Postale 10, 91 rue de la Servette, CH-1211 Genève 7, Suisse

Italy: La Pura Verità, Casella Postale 10349 I-00144 Roma EUR, Italia

Germany: Ambassador College, Postfach 1129, D-5300 Bonn 1, West Germany

Holland and Belgium: Ambassador College, Postbus 444, 3430 AK Nieuwegein, Nederland

Belgium: Le Monde à Venir, B.P. 31, 6000 Charleroi 1, Belgique

Denmark: The Plain Truth, Box 211, DK-8100 Aarhus C, Denmark

Norway: The Plain Truth, Postboks 2513 Solli, N-0203 Oslo 2, Norway

Sweden: The Plain Truth, Box 5380, S-102 46, Stockholm, Sweden

Finland: The Plain Truth, Box 603, SF-00101 Helsinki, Finland

Australia: Worldwide Church of God, P.O. Box 202, Burleigh Heads, Queensland 4220, Australia

India: Worldwide Church of God, P.O. Box 6727, Bombay 400 052, India

Sri Lanka: Worldwide Church of God, P.O. Box 1824, Colombo, Sri Lanka

Malaysia: The Plain Truth, Locked Bag No. 2002, 41990 Klang, Malaysia

Singapore: Worldwide Church of God, P.O. Box 111, Farrer Road Post Office, Singapore 9128

New Zealand and the Pacific Isles: Ambassador College, P.O. Box 2709, Auckland 1, New Zealand

The Philippines: Worldwide Church of God, P.O. Box 1111, MCPO, 1299 Makati, Metro Manila, Philippines

Israel: Ambassador College, P.O. Box 19111, Jerusalem

South Africa: Ambassador College, P.O. Box 5644, Cape Town 8000, South Africa

Zimbabwe: Ambassador College, Box UA30, Union Avenue, Harare, Zimbabwe

Nigeria: Worldwide Church of God, PMB 21006, Ikeja, Lagos State, Nigeria

Ghana: Worldwide Church of God, P.O. Box 9617, Kotoka International Airport, Accra, Ghana

Kenya: Worldwide Church of God, P.O. Box 47135, Nairobi, Kenya

Mauritius: The Plain Truth, P.O. Box 888, Port Louis, Mauritius

THIS BOOKLET IS PROVIDED FREE OF CHARGE BY THE WORLDWIDE CHURCH OF GOD IN THE PUBLIC INTEREST. It is made possible by the voluntary, freely given tithes and offerings of the membership of the Church and others who have elected to support the work of the Church. Contributions are welcomed and gratefully accepted. Those who wish to voluntarily aid and support this worldwide Work of God are gladly welcomed as co-workers in this major effort to preach the gospel to all nations.

373125/8911/2.0